## *Acknowledgements*

To start off, I would like to give thanks to God for the gift of Life. With Life, I can do whatever I want to including writing this book. I wish to thank all the fantastic people that worked for me over the many years. I could not have written this book without the extraordinary life experiences with them. I would like to give thanks to my mom for her willingness to let me try some of my book theories on her. I could not have done it without mom. I have to thank my family for being one of the greatest families ever and of course to my dear friends who have all enriched my life. Lastly, I would like to thank all the wise men and women of the past who wisdom I used to help me have an extraordinary life.

# Table of Contents

# Foreword

I wrote this book to provide guidance to all of my esteemed friends who come to me for help in these trouble times. The book is to remind them that they have all they need to be successful; they just need to be reminded. I was going to call the book "Talk to Yourself", but I do not want people thinking my readers are crazy (smile). I hope this book helps everyone that needs help.

Please read the entire book first, and then go to the website at www.talktothebook.com to get hard copies of all the tools and forms referred to in the book.

I used terms in this book that I made up the definitions. It will be beneficial to know the definitions to understand the meaning. Here, are the terms to know:

**Crap Friends** – People pretending to be your friend, but if one invites them over for dinner, as soon as the individual turns his or her back, the guest will stab the person in the back with their own knife. When people eat a lot of food, they have to crap out the waste. These are friends that one has to get rid of the crap. One can tell by their back stabbing hugs. It is not passionate, and there is no love in the hug. It is as if they need their hands free for stabbing someone.

**Dummy2** – A person like being dumb so much the first time that he or she is coming back again.

**Instant Happy Switch** – One needs to be able to go from a state of stress or depression to being happy in an instant. Life is good; we have to go to remembering that in zero seconds.

**Laws of the Universe** – The universe has laws in which we all have to follow. For example: Law 1 - Everything in the Universe has a cost; nothing is free. If a person gives to the Universe, then the Universe owes him or her valued things. If a person takes away from the Universe, then he or she owes the Universe. There are ten laws in this book which are in chapter five.

**Life Cycle** – Life can be divided into eight hours segments. Eight hours of sleep, eight hours of work and eight hours of life. Look at the life cycle to see if your life is out of balance.

**Life Focus** – Where is your focus in life and is that focus in line with your goals. What gets attention in your life?

**Life Math Function** – Could have plus would have plus should have equals did not. Someone did not do it. Stop talking about it and move on (this is one of the Laws of the Universe).

**Life Surveys** – There should be a lot of lists in individuals' lives that gives one feedback. Use that feedback to have an extraordinary life. We call them surveys because we are going to use the information collected to improve one's lives.

**Money Fairies** – Mythical creatures (meaning I made it up) that bring strapped for cash people money out of the goodness of their hearts. All people have to do is sit around and wait for the "money fairy" to bring them money.

**Quick-Sand Friends (QSF)** – Are friends going down and taking people down with them.

**Self-Evaluation** – What does one think of his or her life? What does one likes with his or her life, and what needs to change?

**Side Rant** – Similar to a side bar; sometimes, I will interrupt the paragraph to talk about my life experiences, but hopefully it makes the book more entertaining.

**Standard of Friends** – Which friend is your standard on which all other friends must meet? Define what level each friend is on. Are they close friends, distance friends and so on? The individual will set the standards and the definition.

**Taking Crazy 101 &102** – We hear that old saying all the time; doing the same thing and expecting different results. Some people seem to go to school and take classes on being crazy.

**The Wait List** – Things that are not in your focus should be put on a waiting list until the individual can get to it.

**"University of You"** – If a person wants to learn something, it is up to that person to learn it.

**Your Universe** – Follow God example; your life is your universe and the individual controls who is in and who is out.

To begin this journey all one needs is a Life to live, Love to fuel the heart, and Time to spend.

LIFE                           LOVE                           TIME

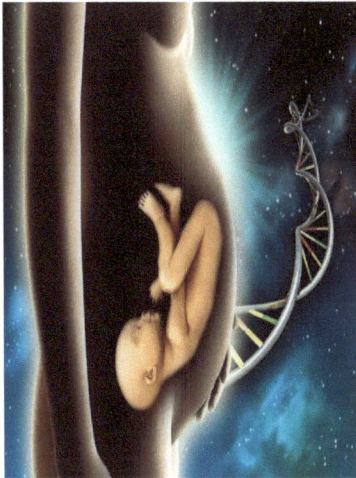      

# Introduction

To start out, let me give a little background on myself, and then I will explain why I wrote this book. I am an identical twin born in a small Florida town. I grew up there until I went to college in Los Angeles, CA. After graduation, I did not just want to be a normal manager. I wanted to understand the philosophy of the people that I managed. Over the next twenty plus years, I imparted a lot of my knowledge to my employees. As the recent recession hit many of my former employees and friends called me for advice. I remember talking to one of my former employee and telling her about some of the other times that the economy was in recession, and we survived. I told her that I should have written all the other times down so that they would have listened to me. For some reason, when things are in print, people believe it more. I thought, what is stopping me from writing it down now, so ten years from now this book will be a reminder of this crisis. This way, I can convey my wisdom to them without being there. In addition, I could use this book as a reminder for myself of how to overcome difficult times.

While many are failing under the crisis, my happy life continues. I am not saying that I am not having a hard time, but my quest for life is still there and my appreciation of time is more apparent now than ever. It is this attitude that has kept me happy. If I can get the individual to this attitude, then he or she will be happy too.

## Life

There are three extremely powerful things to learn in order to be truly happy. The first is Life itself. God gift to us is Life! We get to experience everything from birth to death including joy and despair and everything in between that Life throws at us. Without Life, we are dead. The key thing to understand is that as long as one has Life, any and everything is possible. A person can be in an extremely distressing situation right now, but as long as that person is alive, he or she will have the opportunity to change their situation. For that reason, Life is the world's most precious gift. This is the first step to your self-improvement. A person knowing how precious Life is will not waste his or her Life; therefore, that person will get more out of Life. This whole book is about improving your life. Read it with that in mind and one will benefit tremendously from this book.

## Love

While Life is the most valuable thing period (because if a person is dead, nothing else matters), Love seems to be the most valuable thing to the living. We all need to be loved, and when we are; we are ecstatic. A person would do anything for love including give up life. Someone could argue that love is the most valuable thing, but without life, there is no love. What is the most that a person can love? Has anyone ever loved everyone they possible can? Jesus, I guess! Can we live like Jesus and love everyone? That is hard to do. What about loving just the people that are in ones' own personal universe? That is what this book will help achieve;

create Your Universe so that it will contain the people that will love the individual and the individual loves.

## **Time**

Time is the third most valuable thing in people lives. Once time passes, there is no getting it back. A wasted hour is worth way more than sixty minutes; because once that time goes away, there is no getting it back. It becomes invaluable. No matter how rich people are, they cannot buy time. Time sometimes seems to be the most important, but while a person would do anything to get more time, he or she would give up time for love. If a person is dead, time and love does not matter. The key thing to remember is that Life, Love and Time are the most valuable things in the world. They are extremely close in priority, as this book will address in later chapters. Now, that one understands the priority of Life, Love, and Time, the rest of this book will teach one how to use this information to live an extraordinary life!

# *Chapter 1*

## Self-Evaluation

"Self-Improvement, what is my motivation?"

## **Life Surveys**

People may call them Life Lists, but for the purpose of this book we will refer to them as surveys; because we want one to prepare lists and analyze the information for their benefit.

Each chapter will require one to complete surveys which will not only be a source of information, but reminders of things to do or not do. I know this book requires a lot of lists, but lists have been around for centuries and the wisdom of the past tells us to write it down because if we do not, we will forget. For example, when I go to the grocery store with a list of all the things I want. I get everything on the list every time. Think about that! One hundred percent execution, so a person would think that I would take a list every time, right? We all know the answer to that question. Just the other day, I went to the store for some milk and left the store with everything but milk. Why would I do that if I have a fool proof way of remembering things? The bad part about that is with today's technology; I can put the list in my cell phone which I have with me all the time. One of the key things that we need to do is use technology to improve life and focus. We will talk about that in later chapters.

## Self-Evaluation – Life Survey (SE)

What does one think of him or herself? This is the key to your happiness. If one cannot be satisfied with him or herself, he or she is not going to be happy in life! Making one happy is the main goal of this book. I hope everyone who reads this book wants to be happy. If a person does not want to be happy, then that person needs more help than this book can give. That person should seek professional help. However, for the rest of us who seek self-enlightenment, we will start with the self-evaluation.

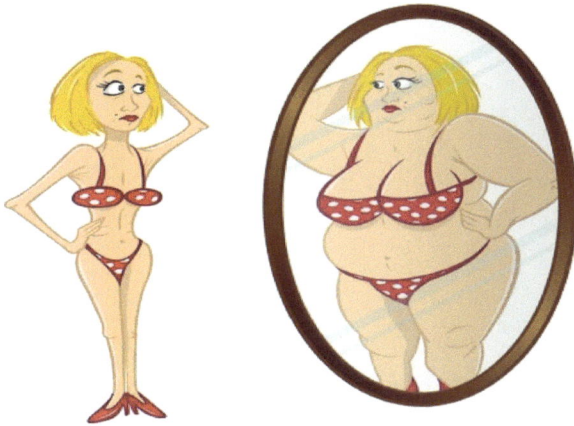

"Does this mirror make me look fat?"

## Image

Your image is the first thing that people see, so let us start with that. There is a self–evaluation form where one will list the "You Now" and the "Ideal You". Decide on the "Ideal You". Remember be realistic. Deciding to change is easy, just doing it is difficult. Think about it, who is the best dress person at work. How much more a person would have to do to out dress that person? Same thing for your friends; what will it take to out dress them? How hard is it to develop a workout program, set a hair appointment or go shopping and buy new clothes? Do not let money keep a person from having fun; it is your responsibility to find a way. Work some overtime or sell something, but if your image is not worth investing in, I do not know what is. Maybe, start with a simple goal like not being the worst dress in the room. Only the individual know what they want to look like, so they have to decide what they want to do. Before beginning work on the self-improvement, we need to know where individuals are at right now. We are going to map out your life.

# Life Map

**"Hit the road Jack"**

People have to know where they are, to get direction to where they are going. To do this, we need to map out your life to find out where the individuals are, and where they would like to go. The individuals will be their own navigation system. We have all watched a comedy show on TV where someone asks the beautiful model; what she does not like about her body? She then lists a lot of things and we all laugh, because we think that she is perfect. Sometime, we can be ourselves own worst critic. Not in this book, one will be your own best friends. Think about it, how many times a slim girl says that she is fat. Self-deprecation is not your friend, so it is not going to be invited in this book. Instead, when we look at a self-evaluation, we are going to look at what we can improve and what is already positive.

At first, it will seem like a lot of hard work, but if people are not willing to work hard for themselves, they would not be reading a self-help book.

**"Yeah, free car wash and a rainbow"**                    **"It is raining, my day is ruined"**

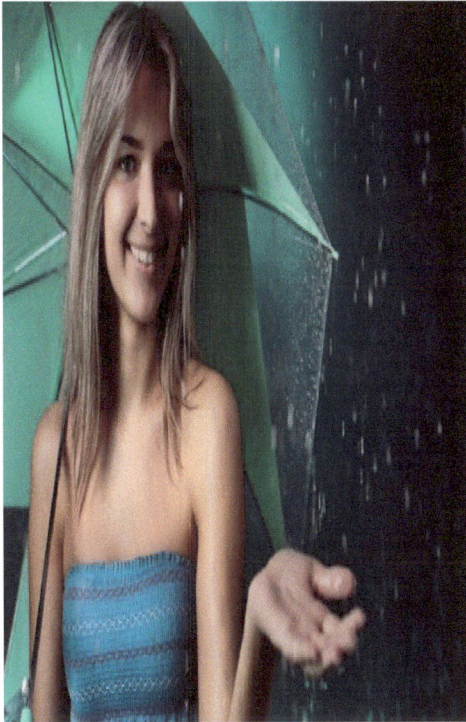

Before we begin, one needs to determine what personality he or she is, positive or negative. What is the difference?  A negative person wakes up and sees that it is raining and says "my day is going to be ruined" and lives a ruined day.  The positive person wakes up and sees that it is raining and says "Yeah! Free car wash and a rainbow" and uses the time he would have use to wash his car doing something else.  Hopefully, one will fall closer to the positive person side.  If not, this book should get them there.  Let us get started with the self-evaluation.

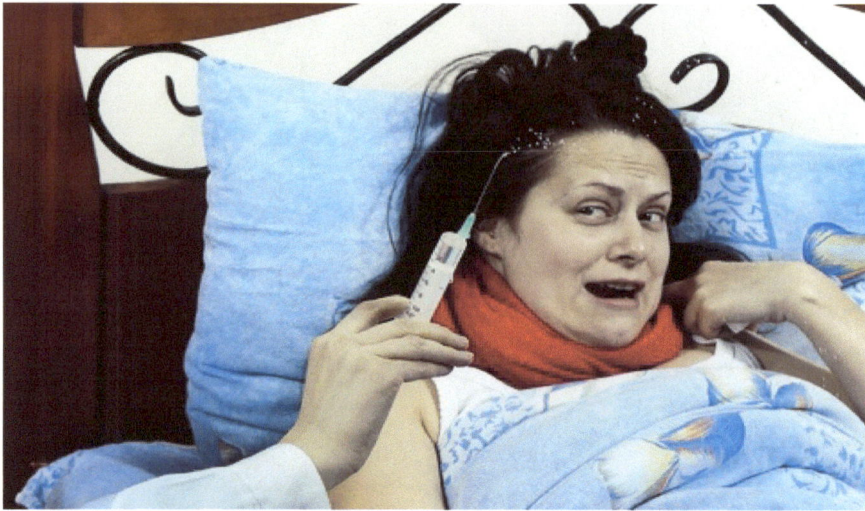

## Life Surveys

To get started, look at the example Life Survey (SE1) – Self-Evaluation. The self-evaluation form is in two sections, Positive and Need to Improve. We capped the form at five things because we do not want to get too negative. For every "Need to Improve" item, one must have an equal number of Positive items (see example).

**Self-Evaluation**

| <u>Positive</u> | <u>Need to Improve</u> |
|---|---|
| 1. Positive Person | 1. Gut – big belly! |
| 2. Family Man | 2. Workaholic |
| 3. Many close friends | 3. Exercise Program |
| 4. Good Christian | 4. Education |
| 5. Great Heart | 5. Insomniac |

We all have some positive things about us that we like.  Let us look at some examples and see how we work on identified issues.

1. Gut – big belly!

   a. Exercise program designed for the gut (sit ups).

   b. Join a gym with a buddy.

   c. Diet.

   d. Surgery – last alternative.

2. Workaholic

   a. Make a list of duties that one can assign and delegate them.

   b. Put an alert on my computer and telephone for when it is time to leave work.

   c. Plan social events after work so that one has to leave on time.

   d. Have a family night after work.

Try to get some positive things first. For example, Ted is a demanding manager and his employees think that he is a pain in the butt. However, Ted's boss thinks that he is the "poop" that does not stink. He is a workaholic, and he is on the fast track to another promotion. In this case, Ted would have a positive and a need to improve all at the same time. Ted just need to figure out how he can be less demanding to his employees and keep the productivity. It is that simple. Maybe create a "team leader" to do some of the follow up, which will give him more time to spend with his family. The individual will be creating a list using the template provided, Life Survey (SE1). Remember there is no right or wrong answers. This is your life.

## **Control What One Can Control**

The first thing one has to learn is to control what they can control. Worrying about things that one cannot control will cause them to have a short life or a long painful one. There are many things in life that are out of your control; however, there are a lot of things that we can control like if we get upset over something or not. For example, I had a business meeting at eight (8) a.m. in the morning. I left my house at six (6) a.m. giving me two hours to get to work. I get about a quarter of the way there and traffic on the freeway just stopped. As the clock got closer to eight (8) a.m., I got more and more upset thinking that everyone is going to think that I did not know how important the meeting is. I then decided to call work and let them know that I was not going to make the meeting. The administrative assistant told me that I was the fourth person to call and that the meeting will be at ten (10) a.m. I thought all that stress for nothing. Being in traffic was out of my control. What was in my control was the choice not to get upset.

Now, let us look at the second self-evaluation form that individuals will need to complete.

Life Survey (SE2) – Self-Evaluation 2

| **You Now** | **Ideal You** |
|---|---|
| Weight – 185 | Weight – 175 |
| Appearance – Good | Appearance – Great |
| Worker – Workaholic | Worker – Quality worker |
| God – Need work | God – Stronger relationship with God |

Taking a look at the example, this person does not have a lot of things to improve.

Let us see how the person in the example can get to the "Ideal You":

1. Weight – first set a goal or time table to lose the ten pounds. For example, over the next three months, that is three and one third pounds per month. Next, set a plan on how to lose weight. Let us use the one we all use; start exercising every day and cut down on high calorie foods. Next, join a gym with a friend who will help one go every day. Now, one is problem solving for the "Ideal You".

2. Appearance – Maybe treat yourself and go buy some new stylist clothes that one can wear to work or around people who use to seeing one dress down. All the great compliments that the individuals are going to get will be a big motivator to dress nicer. People will be surprise how opinion change just by seeing someone cleaned up.

3. God – Going to religious events like a house of worship. This person can also do charity work and pray more. Do things with other religious people so that their moral influence can play a part in building character.

Now that we see what the goal is, please review the Life Survey (SE2) in chapter eight. Forms can also be found on the website at www.talktothebook.com.

## Life Cycle

What is a Life Cycle? Your 24 hours day can be broken up into three cycles, Eight (8) hours for sleep, Eight (8) hours for work and Eight (8) hours for life (fun, family). Please take a look at Life Survey (LC) example.

Life Cycle (LC)

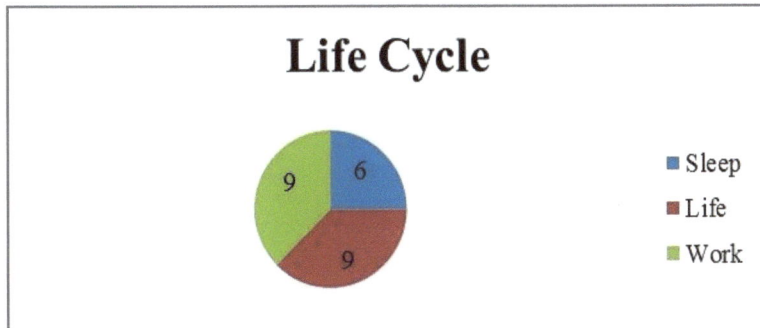

In this example, the person only gets six hours of sleep. For this person to get his life in order, he needs to increase his sleep hours by two hours a day. He could do this by using sleep aides or meditating; however, he would still need to reduce at least one of the other two cycles to get the two hours back. They do not make a twenty-six hour day (although one sometimes wish they would). Some of the ways that he can reduce the work hours are delegate some of his work duties, set the timer on his cell phone, or computer to alert him when it is time to leave work. He can also schedule life events right after work which forces him to leave work on time.

Side Rant: Driving to work goes into what category? That is up to the individual, but because I have a long drive to work that would increase my work hours; I classify driving to work as Life Time. I put all of my favorite songs onto my music player, and then made some CDs with those songs on it. I listen to CDs in the car while driving to work. Think about it, driving to work while listen to your all-time favorite songs. When else would a person have time to sit down and enjoy this? I turned a negative into a positive. Now, if I can just fix that road rage thing (smile).

One now gets the point of the Life Cycle. The individual is ready to do his or her own Life Cycle. Pull out Life Survey (LC) at the end of the book and complete your Life Cycle. Remember this is for your average work week and does not include weekends. Everyone should be using the weekend to enjoy life, and if he or she is not doing that; how to do those things are in a later chapter. Whenever one feels that his or her life is out of balance, do a Life Cycle survey.

### Life Survey (FS1 & 2)

The Family and Friend Surveys are the next forms that need to be complete. These forms will require feedback from your family and friends. Most of us should be able to be honest with a self-evaluation, but we may see ourselves with either too polite or too embarrassed eyes; so the old saying that family and friends will always tell the truth should hold true. One is going to use Life Surveys FS1 and FS2 to get opinions from family and friends of what they think about the individual. If one cannot handle criticism, then skip this part, but feedback from others is an invaluable tool for self-improvement. However, we do not want one to lose close friends over this. Use your judgment. We will start with Life Survey (FS1) Friend Survey.

## Life Survey (FS1) Friends Survey

People can make up their own questions; just do not make them too personal.  Your true friends and family should be able to answer the questions truthfully.  The form is at the end of the book (see example).

1.  What Kind of person do you think that I am?

    A.  Positive

    B.  Negative

    C.  Neutral

    D.  Assume crash position

2.  Would you say that I am a _____?

    A.  Giver

    B.  Taker

    C.  Other, please describe

    D.  I do not care

Make sure to choose friends whom opinions mean something.  I suggest that the individual takes them to lunch or dinner as a reward for helping them.  After getting several friends to provide feedback, then get feedback from your family.  Again, pick family members that one values their opinions.  With family, the individual can conduct the interview over the phone if they are out of town.  When one is ready to do the family interview, use form Life Survey (FS2) in chapter eight.

# *Chapter 2*

Life Focus

**Which way should I go?**

## **Plan Progression**

Now that, one knows where he or she is going, it is time to draw the path or roads to your success. To do this, we must first determine who the "boss of you" is. People hear it all the time. Someone says "you are not the boss of me". It is essential that the individuals manage their own time because this is a vital component to controlling your focus. If your business is controlling your life, then talk to your boss. If your spouse is controlling your time; talk to him or her. If they love the individual, they should be willing to give control back. One needs to be in control of his or her universe because he or she has to make life altering decisions.

As the individual works on his or her focus, there is a lot of wisdom from the past that we use. We will discuss that next.

## "There is nothing that I can do tomorrow, today".

That is one of my favorite saying.  I will not let tomorrow problems ruin today.  This book is about not blaming other people for problems in your life, but taking control of your life so that the individuals are the bosses of their lives.  That way if one is not enjoying life, it will be their fault.  Slow things down and get it together; your life is not going anywhere.  Enjoy the things that today brings; sunshine, love ones and life surprises.  Work on tomorrow problems, tomorrow.

## The Wait List

Put it on a waiting list if someone asks one to do something that is not on his or her Focus List.  The individuals have to do an instant valuation on the things they do before they do them.  A person should be working on his or her focus first, but if someone else wants one to do something and it is outside his or her focus, he or she has to put it on a waiting list in order of significant to the individual.  Your focus would be the highest priority and the wait list would be the lowest priority.

If anything, take all the lessons that people learned so far and go out and have a better life.   Do not be a go to guy or girl for everyone but yourself.  Make sure what the individuals are doing is in their focus.  Nothing is significant enough to put in front of your Focus List.  Remember, your focus will drive your life and your life decisions.

We have one last thing to consider before starting on the Life Focus list.  Remember the saying; control what one can control.  For example, Ted's company closed down, and Ted had to take a job making less money.  Ted has to stop living the life he wanted because he just does not make enough money.  The company closing was out of his control, but getting stress out over not being able to pay a credit card company is under his control.  Now a person should always pay his bills if he can afford it, but if something out of your control happens, your Life Focus will become even more valuable.  Because if we lose focus because of tough times, we will never get that wasted time back.

Talk to some elderly people and ask them what they would give to get those wasted years back.  Keep things in perspective, that credit card company quarterly press released said that they made three billion dollars (that's billion with a "b") in the last quarter (that is three months profits).  They are not going to go out of business because Ted did not make a payment for a month or two, but yet, he cannot sleep at night worrying about how he is going to pay them. He should be calling or writing the credit card company to tell his story.  He may be surprised how they are willing to work with him.  In Ted's world, the credit card companies answers to him. Ted is the boss of his world and guess who is going to decide if they get paid or not.

Control what one can control.  Do not stop life because of a crisis.  That is when a person needs an extraordinary life the most!   Use Life Survey (PL) – Problem List and write down the problems that one has to solve and deal with them one at a time when the individual budget time to deal with them.  The form is in chapter eight, and it is available on the website at www.talktothebook.com.

## Life Focus

Now we are ready to start on your Life Focus. Remember this will drive your life decisions. The things on your list will get attention. Let us look at an example before we start:

What are the most valuable things in your life! This will guide your life and give focus.

Life Focus – Who or what is number 1?

1. God
2. Family
3. My Life
4. Friends
5. Career

The above person has his focus for life. God is the most valuable thing, so he should live a life that represents God as the top priority. If he is not, then his focus needs to change. A person cannot say God is the most powerful thing in his life, and live the life of someone whom it seems as if God is last in his life. That would be the sign of an unhappy person. Remember, the key to this working is to be honest. If "You" are the number one thing in your life then put "You" as the number one thing, and pleasing yourself will become your number one focus. For example, God cannot be put first in your focus if one does not like religious events, he or she never prays and he or she breaks most of the Ten Commandments every month. That person would have to change everything for God to be his top priority in life. Not to say that people do not want to change, but your focus has to be realistic for one to be happy.

Another example would be for a person with that focus being a workaholic. He should realize that his family is the second most valuable thing to him. He needs to take time away from work (which is number five) and give that extra time to his family (number two). All he has to learn to do is follow his Life Focus. What is beneficial to him, make sure he keeps that in focus. That way he makes sure that he put a priority on what is valuable to him. Anytime an individual feels that he or she is getting away from his or her focus, work to get back to it. When focus changes over time, just redo your Focus List. Now review the Life Survey (LF) Life Focus and began completing it. Remember your Focus List will be the most influential list that one will make because it will drive your life decisions.

## Life Goals

Life Goals – If a person is going on a lifelong trip, one has to have some attractions that he or she wants to see. These are the things that will make up your Life List or Life Goals. These are the things that a person wants to do while he or she is living. We heard it call the bucket list or things to do before we die list, but we will call it the Life List because that is what it is. The individual is going to check off events as he or she does them. This is the fun part!

I can remember being in the mortgage industry when things took off. We could do no wrong, so we thought. Life was incredible! My Life List was long and filled with an impressive list of things to do. I had my Life List, and I had reminders all over the place to remind me to do things. For example, I kept a picture of the Eiffel Tower on my computer to remind me to plan a trip to Paris. My list was aggressive with things like the Super Bowl, NBA Finals, World Series and the Grammys. Not only did I go to all those events, I remember my friend from Hawaii calling me because Madonna was playing in Los Angeles and she wanted to see her. I told her that I did not want to see a Madonna concert. She then said to me that it was on her Life List. After that, how could I refuse? So I bought tickets, and we all went to the concert. I remember telling someone that life must be incredible if I am doing things on my friend's Life List.

The main point is that in making that list, we all knew what we wanted in life. So when life presented an opportunity to us, we not only knew it was an opportunity, we knew we had to take advantage of it. That is the whole purpose of the Life List; to remind one of the things that they want to do because sometime, life is so busy that we need a list!


One thing to keep in mind is to keep the list dynamic, meaning that it can change, but do not be afraid to put some extremely difficult things on the list. As we go through life, a person priority may change so his or her lists will change with it.


I remember having one of my favorite singers, Sade' on my list of concerts to go to, but I had to go to my girlfriend friend's birthday party instead of the concert. After the concert, the singer stops performing at concerts. I was so upset that I would not get to see one of the artists in concert on my list. I left it on the list just in case life presented me with an opportunity. It did ten years later, when Sade' was performing at an event in Southern California. It was a fantastic concert, by the way. Remember, this is a Life List, so it does not have to be something to do in the next few months.

Please look at the example of a Life List:

## Life List

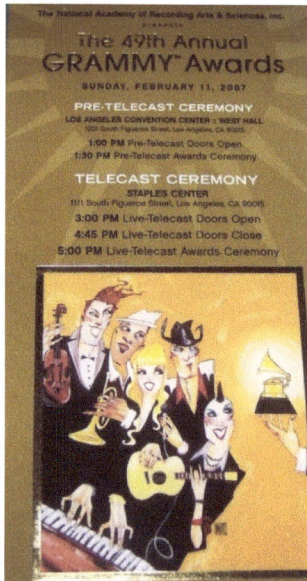

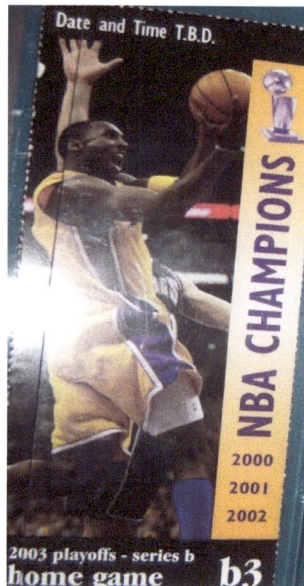

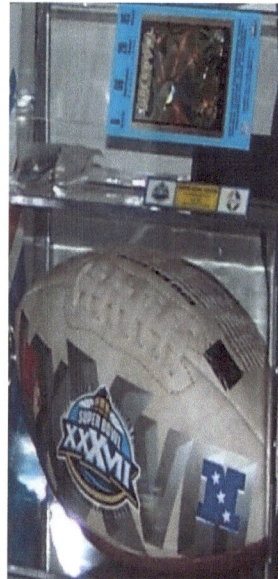

**Grammy, NBA Finals and the Super Bowl.**

| Events to go to | Dates went to events |
|---|---|
| 1. Super Bowl | TBD |
| 2. World Series | TBD |
| 3. NBA Finals | TBD |

| **Concerts to go to** | **Dates went to concerts** |
|---|---|
| 1. Grammy | TBD |
| 2. America Music Award | TBD |
| 3. Sade' Concert | TBD |

| Places to go | Dates went to place |
| --- | --- |
| 1.  Paris | TBD |
| 2.  Venice | TBD |

| Major things to do | Dates |
| --- | --- |
| 1.  Get Married and Have Children | TBD |
| 2.  Buy House | TBD |

This is the one list where there are no limits!  This is your Life List, so the individuals set the limits.  Remember the key is to keep this list where one sees it every day.  In addition, to that have a reminder around the house and at work.  For example, I bought a couple of model cars, and put one by my computer at home and one by my computer at work to remind me not only what I was working for, but what I wanted.  When I bought the car, I was so excited and thought that I could do any and everything on my list.  Remember the list is going to be what the individual wants to do.  Whatever it is, one should be able to get a picture of it, and put it somewhere to remind them of what they want.  Go to chapter eight and get Life Survey (LL) and complete it.  Remember, No Limits!  The forms can be also be downloaded on the website at www.talktothebook.com.

## Organize your life to match your Life Lists

Now that, one has his or her Life Map and Life Goals; one must be his or her own navigation system.  What is the number one thing on your Focus List?  Plan your life activities so that they are in line with your focus.  For example, if the family is the number one thing in your life, plans some family only events. A person could have family movie day on Saturday, family game night on Tuesday and so far and so on. Since the family is first, your Life Focus will be on doing things with the family. Obviously, that person has to get his or her family to cooperate, but that should not be a problem because if a person has family first, that person must have a close and loving family. People with a dysfunctional family will not usually put family that high on their list.

Now all one has to do is start the trip of your life!

# *Chapter 3*

## Body, Mind and Soul

"My body is a Holy Temple!"

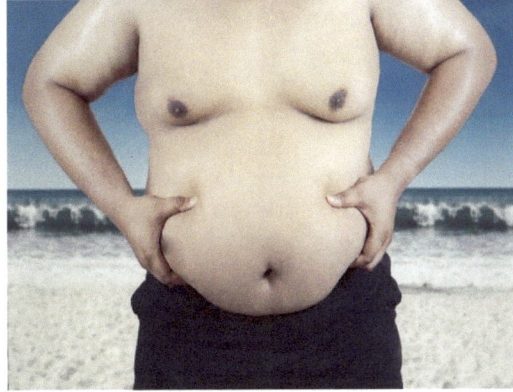

"My body is the world's largest Temple!"

## **Body**

In your self-evaluation, the individual addresses his or her appearance or should have.  Do not worry if one did not because we are going to address it here.  Taking care of your body should be a focus in your life.  People, who smoke their whole life, usually have extremely painful, cancer latent, hospital ridden end of life.  What would they have given to go back in time and not smoke?  Religious or not, a person still have to think of his or her body as a Holy Temple, because if they do not, their last years on earth will be extremely sad and painful.  The sad part is that it does not take much for us to take care of the body.  There is so much guidance out there like exercising, walk every day, and watch your diet.  It is worth your time to discuss it with your doctor or some health care professionals. Learn what is right for your body. The individual will be able to work on areas that need to be improved.

In the past, people would spend their whole life looking for the fountain of youth. We know today that by exercising every day, we not only improve the present but the future life. Think about it, if someone told a person that he or she will have a much better life by exercising every day, that person would be foolish not to do it. The individual has to put exercising somewhere on his or her focus list. A person cannot do self-improvement without doing some form of exercise. Sorry, but it is a requirement.

**"My weight loss program"**

## Image

The first thing that people see is your image.  Are they going to be looking at the best person possible? We cannot do a self-evaluation without talking about your appearance.  Guess what; taking care of your appearance will improve your image.  I am not saying that one has to wear a suit on your days off, but what is wrong with looking good for those who see the individual on the weekends.  If a person cares about his or her appearance, looking fresh every day is a required task.   Girls are way ahead of guys in taking care of their image.  If a person needs to lose weight, then lose the weight.  Work toward the "Ideal You".

There are five things that one must check on a regular basis:

1.  Blood Pressure

2.  Blood Sugar

3.  Cholesterol

4.  Weight relative to your body size (BMI)

5.  Your Appearance

Check with your medical provider as they will have a wealth of resources for this.  We provide a chart to track your numbers in chapter eight.  See Life Survey form "MED".  The form can also be downloaded at www.talktothebook.com.

## Mind

Maybe even more valuable than your body is your mind. There are so many things that one can do to enhance his or her mind. Take classes online if one has a busy schedule. There has been considerable advancement in technology especially in computers. Take some online computer classes so the individual does not miss out on the technological revolution that is going on. Learn a foreign language. One can even take that online. Do things that will improve your mind. One of my favorite things to do is to meditate. I highly recommend it. I am not trying to turn someone into Gandhi, but I suffer from insomnia and meditating has helped me. A person needs to be the "University of You". There are things that the individual always wanted to learn, but just never got around to it. Learn it now.

## Soul

A person needs God! It makes no sense not to believe in God. Life is going to throw some tough challenges your way. A normal person may not be able to handle it, but a person with a supreme being to help him or her will be able to overcome anything. I like to share with everyone a poem that I wrote in college. "What is impossible? If not something believed cannot be done, and when someone believes in all things, then impossible is none". With us things are impossible "but with God all things are possible"[1]. I am going to share something that should make believing in God an absolute. A person is dead way longer than they are alive. Wise people will make sure that their place of death is a pleasant one. If people are right and nonbelievers end up in hell because they did not invest any time in seeing if there is a God, their afterlife will be a terribly unpleasant one. Think about it, people who died five hundred years ago would have been in hell for five hundred years. Scary!

Let us look at it this way, we all plan and save for retirement so that the elderly years will be pleasant. We asked the brokers questions about the yield on the money, how safe it is, and we want monthly statements to verify it. We invest time and effort to make sure we have a happy retirement. A person who does not save up or plan for retirement will have a tough life after they retire. We would say that person was truly not wise. Remember, everyone is going to be dead a lot longer than they are going to be retired. Does one think it is worth the investment of his or her time to do some research on rather there is a God or not? I am not telling someone to pick a religion. I believe God is the God of all. Rather a person calls him God or some other name; he is still God of everyone.

Most of the prophets spoke in parables because they wanted a thinking man. Invest in your death! Take the time to study God for yourself. Ask questions of religious leaders and make sure it makes sense. People investing their life savings with Bernie Madoff did not ask the right questions. Now that, he spent all the money; it is too late to ask those questions because they cannot get their money back.

Death works the same way. The time to ask questions is when people are alive because once they die; dead people do not have money. Being a Christian, I think that the reason that Christ did not just give us the meaning of life or write the Book of Christ is because he wanted us to find out for ourselves. Think about it, how many times have we seen some religious group do something that is so far away from their faith, but yet these people think they are the most faithful to their religion.

Remember, this is your life; only the individual is responsible for his or her decisions. It does not matter whether a person is rich or poor because all the money on earth will not buy anyone a drink of water in Hell, and Hell does not accept ATM Cards, Visa, MasterCard or American Express! If that does not scare one enough to start investing some time in finding God, then I do not know what will. That is the best advice that I can give. I know this is a self-help book and not a religious book, but the people who have strong faith have been able to overcome the most difficult situations. We want one to be able to handle anything that life throws at him or her, but a person needs God to do that! Try to follow one of my saying when choosing a religion, "there are some questions that we must answer, and then there are some answers that we must question". Good luck!

## Pick a Charity

Doing things for others is morally right, but also makes that person feel better about him or herself. One needs to champion a charity. It does not have to be one of the many organized charities. It could be just helping the neighbor get her medicine from the drug store. Do something that will affect a person life and is measurable, other than writing a check. Your goal is to affect someone life for the better.

I remember as a teenager people in the neighborhood that had problems paying their house payments would have these "block parties" and charged $10 per person. They must have raised at least $1,000 by the number of people that attended. If a person with a spacious house can organize something like that, it will certainly help the many people having trouble paying their house payments. That would be an example of something one could measure how many people he or she helped, and the individual gets to party as a bonus. Think outside the box to help people. These are tough times. People will appreciate it way more now than ever, and the individual will be on his or her way to making him or herself a better person.

# Chapter 4

## Write Yourself a Happy Next

Happy Next List

What is one waiting for to do the things that he or she wants to do? We hear stories all the time of people in plane crashes or thought they were going to be in a plane crash. They use their last few minutes on earth calling love ones and just wishing that they can spend one more day with them. They are not calling work to tell their bosses that their report is not going to be done. Please, do not wait for a plane to crash to realize what is precious. Put your focus together and do what is beneficial to one now.

There will always be people better off and worst off, but one has no control over their lives, just your own. If a person wakes up and sees that it is raining, there is nothing he or she can do about the rain. I guess someone can try to do a rain dance in reverse, but I doubt that will work. It will just make that person look foolish. The point is not to bring any self-fulfilling prophecies. For example, a person wakes up and sees it is raining, so he thinks that his day is going to be bad. He spends the day looking for the terrible things that day will bring, and never sees the positive things all around him. He predicted a miserable day, so his mind will make his prediction come true. One has to get in the habit of looking for the good; rather it be the love in people, the joy of living another day. One has another day to praise God, and to spend time with someone who may not be here much longer.

I used to live in Hawaii and after each rain storm would come the most beautiful rainbows in the sky. It got to the point that whenever it was raining, I would always look for the beautiful rainbows. That is the way we need to start thinking. When life is pouring down on us, look for the rainbows or know that after the rain, comes the rainbows.

Try to do something fun every day! In fact, let us fill out the fun list right now so that the individual does not have to think about it. When one wants to do something fun, just pull out your fun list and pick one or more of the items. I try to do at least two things a day. Look at Life Survey (FL) Fun List example, and complete the form in chapter eight.

Happy Beach Day!

Happy Next List (Fun List)

1.  Spa Day

2.  Go to the Beach

3.  Lunch  or dinner with friends

4.  Watch a funny movie or show that make me laugh

5.  Go to a sporting event or social event

6.  Golf Day

7.  Go Shopping

8.  Call Mom

This is a handy list for when a person has a miserable day and needs a happy next.  He or she does not have to think, just pick one.  Only the individual knows what he or she likes, but something that one can do every day is to watch something funny that makes him or her laugh. One can watch TV shows, the internet, or some fun DVDs. I downloaded all my favorite comedies shows and can watch them whenever I want to or need to laugh.

## Define Happy

What makes us happy? What is the definition of your happiness? That is for the individual to decide. We need to define happiness so that we know when we reach it. For example, if Karen says that she will be happy once she gets married. Once she gets married, she should be happy by her own definition. Life keeps us so busy that we sometime need someone to tell us to shut up and be happy. Please see Life Survey form "DH" in chapter eight to define your idea of being happy.

## To Do List

We all have to do lists; however, we usually put all the things that we hate to do on them. What if we put things we want to do on the list? I have a check list in my cell phone that I use daily. I have incorporated my fun list in my To Do list. I have at least two to three fun things on my list every day. If your phone does not have a To Do list, then there are some online. Remember to put some things from your Happy Next list each day. Another tip is to list a few things that are one time things. For example, fixing the leaking pipe in the bathroom would be a one-time thing.

## The Senses

We all know of the five senses: hearing, taste, seeing, smell, and touch. Let us talk about the five senses. We will talk about how to keep your senses content and thereby keeping one happy. The senses are the body way of getting feedback of what is going on in your life. Happy feedback makes people happy, so let us talk about that.

## Seeing (Sight)

Can people control what they see? Sometime people can and remember the saying "control what one can control". At home and even at work, one can control what he or she sees. Keep things that one thinks is beautiful all around them. If one has a family picture where everyone is happy, and every time he or she looks at it, it brings the person immense joy! Put that picture somewhere the individual can see it every day. Take one today if one does not have one.

Side Rant - I remember when I was graduating from college. I just finished finals, still working my two part time jobs, family coming out for graduation, and interviewing for my future jobs after college. I was so stress, and I still had to take my graduation pictures. I showed up late for the pictures and set down and told the man that I was in a hurry, so take the pictures quickly. I set there for several minutes and waited for him to take the picture. At first, I thought that he was not taking the pictures because I told him to hurry, so I waited a few more minutes.

Finally, I asked him what is wrong. He replied, "You are graduating from college after four long years; you should be extremely happy, and I am not going to take the picture until you are smiling". I thought; he is right! I am graduating from college! All of a sudden, an exceedingly happy feeling came over me, and I begin to smile uncontrollably. I had no thought of stress in my life, just the excitement of knowing that I had made it through four years of college. He then took pictures and his comment was that my "now smile" was the best that he had taken all week. To this day, I keep one of those pictures to remind me to stop and enjoy life now; just like I did in my pictures. I learned that I had an instant happy switch.

One could have pictures of your favorite movie stars, devoted friends and family, or even motivational things like pictures of things to do. For example, I kept a post card of Hawaii on my office wall to remind me that I wanted to go to Hawaii. The employees that came into my office joked that the guy in the picture on the beach was me. I went to Hawaii once a month. The point is to keep things around that makes your eyes happy!

## Hearing

With today's technology, a person can make a list of songs that go back in time. My music player contains my favorite songs of all times going back to when I was a kid. I then burn CDs to listen to on my drive to work. People must think I am crazy as I drive to work singing my favorite songs every day. When does a person get to listen to all of their favorite songs? See how easy it would be for one to do this. I promise this will bring one joy! I even have a playlist for when I work out at the gym. All the people there see a happy guy who sometimes sings as he works out.

## Taste

This is the easiest one to make happy!  Just go out and get all ones' favorite foods and have them available to the individual when he or she needs it.  Post a list of your favorite foods on your refrigerator.  That way everyone knows what to get when they go shopping.  Eating (along with sex) is one of the few things in life that is pure pleasure and can be done every day.  So far so easy!  Let us look at the rest of your senses.


## Touch

Who does not like to be touched in the right way?  Sex is one of the few things that a person can do every day which is pure pleasure, and there are remarkably few things in life better than having sex with someone that the person love.  I should not have to say it, but having more sex will make everyone happier.   One can also have sex alone, but that is a subject for a totally different book (smile).

Who does not want a relaxing massage?  Even if, a person does not have a partner to share a massage with, there are so many spas and massage products out there to bring one immense joy.  Do the ultimate and go to a spa and have whatever treatment that the individual likes.  Although spa treatments can be expensive at the high end spas, there are a number of small spas that are extremely low cost.  Do your homework.  One should know his or her body.  What pleases it?  Write it down and make sure to do it.

## Smelling

Companies have spent billions to create products to make sure people enjoy what they smell. It could be your favorite cologne or perfume; it could be the smell of your favorite food cooking, and we have not even mentioned all of the air freshener products.

Think about it; if a person can keep all five of their senses happy or most of them, that person will be happy!  For example, A man is at home in bed with the love of his life, watching his favorite movie while cuddling, eating his favorite food.  I know that those two people would be extremely happy.  Try it!

# Chapter 5

## Your Universe

"Don't worry about that Karma thing. See, I am taking what I want and nothing has happened to me yet".

## Laws of the Universe

There are laws in the universe that we all must know and follow. Here are the ones that everyone needs to know to understand this book:

1. Everything has a price; nothing is free. If a person gives to the Universe, then the Universe owes him or her, but if a person takes from the Universe, then he or she owes the Universe.

2. A person can only live in one time. He or she can live in the past, present or the future; but not more than one at a time.

3. If a person blames God for all of his problems, then he or she should expect more problems as a punishment for blaming God.

4. Time cannot be bought. Once a person is dead, they are dead – the end.

5. Self-fulfilling prophecies have a way of coming true.

6. Life Math Function – could have plus would have plus should have equal did not.

7. There are things outside of your control.

8. Your body is a temple made up of whatever a person puts into it.

9. Whatever happens happened. Once something happens, it is now in the past.

10. Hell does not take ATM Cards, MasterCard, Visa or American Express.

## God is the Best Example

Now that, the individual has focus and control of your life, it is time to create "Your Universe". The reason we pick "Your Universe" is to follow the best example that we know. God created the Universe, and it has worked for hundreds of billions, maybe hundreds of trillions of years. The way this works is that one will create his or her universe and follow the Laws of the Universe.

Like the earth revolves around the sun, the individual will need to determine who the sun in your life is. Everything revolves around the individual but the sun. The individual revolves around the sun, so the sun in your life will be the most influential people like your parents, spouse or children. Ones' universe is going to revolve around these people. Your earth will be where one will keep family, friends, co-workers and others.

The exciting news is that it is your universe and one can change it whenever he or she wants. Someone is treating the individual wrong, send their butt to Pluto, and it is not even a planet anymore. No one messes with a person in your own universe! Try to be a pleasant ruler of your universe. Now with that being said, the individual will need to list all of the people in his or her life and review those that should be close to the individual and those whom the individual may need to send to Pluto. This is your chance to get rid of those negative people, the Quick Sand Friends (QSF) and the Crap Friends in your life. The friends that do not enrich your life, but bring drama and pain need to go. These so called friends are going down and taking friends with them. This may be the toughest thing to do, but I promise that if a person surround him or herself with nothing, but people who care and are willing to help, that person will be the happiest that he or she can be.

Look at babies. They are always happy because people around them give them nothing but love. I remember speaking to this motivational speaker, and he told me that I had to get rid of the negative people in my life. He said I should surround myself with positive people. As I list all the positive and negative people in my life, one of my closest and I thought best friend was on the negative side. I had known her for many years and maybe spent time with her at least once a month for each of those years. I kept thinking there is no way that I could cut her off, but the more I look at what I would be giving up, the more the case to give up her friendship seems to be the right thing to do.

For example, the reason that I saw her once a month is because she had at least one crisis in her life once a month and always called me or got me involved. Working on her drama, I was taking away time from my life that I could never get back. The more I reasoned with the idea of getting her out of my life, the more it made sense. When I finally made the decision to cut her off (and it was a hard decision), I had all this free time on my hand. I discover traveling and how much I like going places. My life improved immediately. I surrounded myself with people who liked to go places, and we all started going to all the places that we dreamed of. There is no way that I would have been able to do that with that old friend in my life.

Think about it, if one could surround his or her life with nothing but people, who loved and wanted to help him or her be happy, what an extraordinary life it would be. Well, in your own universe, one can. The individual will just have to make some tough decisions, but that is why one is the God of his or her "Universe". Unless they are your children, the individual is not responsible for them. Just like one is the boss of himself; they are the boss of themselves.

## Your Life History in Time

Time is the third most valued thing in your universe. What are the first two? Life and Love! While a person would do anything to get more time, that same person would do everything for love, even give up time. We will cover Love in chapter seven.

Time, no matter how wealthy or poor a person is; they cannot buy a second of time back. We all have one life to live so do not waste it. Ask any elderly person what they would do if they could go back in time. They all would want to go back and do something different. If we do not waste time, it could be ones' best friend. If something in your past is bothering the individual, unless someone builds a time machine, forget about it! Think about it, even if there is a time machine, we could not let people go back in time and fix their mistakes because time would never go forward if we did. If it is hard to forget about, then rewrite your history so that it does not bother the individual anymore.

## Put it in Your Rear View Mirror

When a person is driving, the best way to drive is to keep his or her eyes forward on the road or path in front. Every now and then, that person will look into the rear view mirror. He or she can only do that for a brief time and then all eyes forward again. That is how we need to live life. Always looking forward and keeping both eyes on the path that we choose. Every now and then, we can look in the past, but it should be for an extremely brief time.

If Tom is driving from Florida to California and he is now in Texas. There is no reason for Tom to try to see Florida. If something unpleasant happens, it is now in the past and cannot be changed. We have to move on. Who is the better driver in life, the person that keeps his eyes on the road, or the person that keeps looking into his rear view mirror? A person looks into their rear view mirror. He can only look for a few seconds, or he could get into an accident. Life is that way. Take a quick glance at your history when needed, but all eyes are on life going forward or unpleasant things could happen.

I was in Paris, France, and the tour bus driver was taking us all around town telling us how the illustrious Napoleon built the magnificent city of Paris to protect the French people from their enemies. Her view of Napoleon was way different that the view I got in American schools. Just then, I realized something that would change my life. I now know that history is in the control of the people who tell it. Who can tell your history better than the individual? I do not know about anyone else, but if I am writing my own history, it is going to be a pleasurable one.

So now that one is going to write a magnificent personal history, your future should be an unwritten book that one gets to write or prewrite. <u>If one does not learn anything else from this book, learn this: For anyone to be truly happy, they must have a short term memory on the mistakes in their lives. That way, they never worry about their mistakes because they do not exist anymore.</u>

Side Rant – I remember playing high school football, and we started the year beating the crosstown rival 30 to 0. In the next week game, we had a touchdown lead with a few minutes to go and the opponents were on the two yard line trying to tie the score. We held them out of the end zone on four straight downs and won the game. The defensive effort was the talk of the town. We had another game where the opponent had the ball late in the game at the two yard line, and we held them out three straight downs. They went for it on fourth down, and I missed the tackle, and they scored. I went to the sideline with my head hung down to sit on the bench.

What I forgot is that I also return kickoffs. The coaches were calling for me, but I could not hear anything because of my self-pity. By the time I realized that I was on the kick off team, the coach had grabbed someone else and put him in my place. My replacement did not return kick offs, and of course they kicked the ball to him, and he fumbled it. Me getting upset over the touchdown stop me from focusing on the future. I should have been focusing on running the kickoff back for a touchdown to make up for the score, and everyone would have forgotten my missed tackled. However, by thinking about something in the past, I hurt my present and future. We already established that no one can go back into time; so everyone must always live their life as if it is always going forward because it is! Focus on the future and what to do next. One has to have a short memory in life if he or she wants to move on in his or her life. If something is hard to forget, then rewrite your history so that it does not bother the individual anymore.

### No one can have a bad future!

Now that one knows how to write a positive history; let us prewrite your future. One can go to any place that they want. The individual is writing his or her future or at least prewriting it. The individual can go back to school to learn computers or go on that world cruise that the individual has always dreamed of doing. Prewrite these exciting events in your life by making a Life List. The future is like "Tomorrow", it is always "what happens next". The individual gets to decide at least what he or she wants to do in the future, and doing those things, well, that is what we call living life. One has to believe this in order to go after things previously believed to be out of reach. We all have had times in life where we thought things will not get better, but they did. We just need to be reminded.

Side Rant: I remember talking to a friend, who was going through severe financial problems, and she did not see her way out, but she believed that somehow she was going to have a lot of money just fall into her lap. I remember saying to her, "hey, I just started playing the lottery too, but I do not win more than two dollars". She replied, "I do not play the lottery; I'll have a better chance to be struck by lightning". I thought to myself, at least she is reasonable about something because if she believed that money is just going to drop in her lap, she is Crazy101 and 102.

When we were kids, we used to put a tooth under the pillow expecting that the tooth fairy would bring us some cash. Usually, the tooth fairy did; however as we grew up we stop believing in childish fantasy and realized that there is no such thing as the tooth fairy. As adults, we know that there is no such thing as the "Money Fairy". If we want cash, we have to go out and get it, so unless someone create the "Money Fairies", we have to get money ourselves.

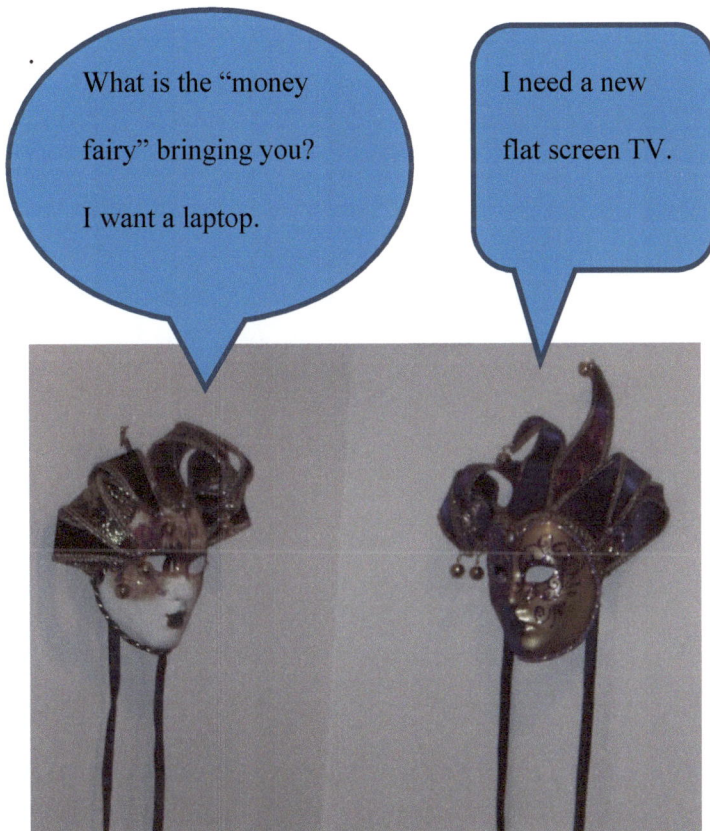

Everyone can have dreams, but unless they go after them, that is all they are dreams. If a person wants to travel to an exotic location and cannot afford it, that person has to find a way to make extra money to make the dream a reality. Trust me; the harder that a person work to make a dream happen, the happier that person will be when the dream becomes a reality.

## Your Universe

Now it is time to write it down and make your universe! The individual is ready to complete the Life Survey (YU) – form in chapter eight. Remember do not put people close that should not be there like Quick Sand Friends. Complete the form now.

## Wisdom of the Past

One of the greatest things getting lost in history is the wisdom of the past. Generations of people would pass down their wisdom to the next generation. The "generation now" thinks that they have to make their own mistakes; when history has shown that learning from other mistakes, especially someone that one respect is the greatest teacher. One of the things that will make us so much better is to learn not just from one's mistakes, but the mistakes of others.

I was lying in my bed watching TV and the CEO of Chrysler came on thanking the American people for bailing out Chrysler. I had a late seventy, early eighty flashback, remembering Lee Iacocca (the then CEO of Chrysler) saying the same things decades ago.

What got me to thinking is when the CEO said that they learned their lesson, and this will never happen again. Lee Iacocca said the same thing on the first bailout of Chrysler. Obviously, we did not learn anything from the first bailout because we bailed them out the second time.

Think about the savings and loans bailout in the eighty's. We just bailed banks out again. However, "fool me once, shame on you, but fool me twice, shame on me"[2], but fool me three times, I guess that saying is yet to be determine. See the point of all the lists now! Write it down so we do not forget!!! That way the next time Chrysler comes for a bailout, "we can say fool me once, shame on you, but fool me twice, shame on me", try to fool me three times, Talk to the Book!

## Life Lessons or Mistakes

We all have heard it called by different names, "school of hard knocks", and "my bad". No matter what a person called it, it means that something wrong happened. There are two ways to look at it. The first, if someone makes a mistake, but can learn from it, it then becomes a life lesson.

For example, a guy cheats on his first girlfriend, and she leaves him. He learns that he has to be honest and trustworthy in a relationship; so with the next girlfriend, he stays honest. That is a life lesson.

A mistake is when he did not learn from the experience and cheated on the next girlfriend. So now we can take that approach to all the "my bad" situations in life. If we learn from them, then they were all life lessons and made us a better person. If we did not learn anything, then they were mistakes.

A person with a lot of life lessons is a wise men or woman, but a person with a lot of mistakes is a fool whose future holds many more mistakes. Live your life and do not be afraid of making mistakes; just learn from them. When a person gets extremely old, he or she will not remember what they did. So in the end, not doing things will cost a person years of lost memories.

One of the main themes is to learn from all mistakes, even if the mistakes were not by us. Knowledge is cheap! There is so much wisdom of the past to use. Trust me; there is much pain and sorrow from learning from your own mistakes. It is so much easier to learn from others mistakes than your own. In the time of Socrates (which was around 400 BC), he said "Employ your time in improving yourself by other writings so that you shall gain easily what others have labored hard for"[3]. That wisdom has been around for a long time. Having wisdom is the sign of a wise person rather they learned the wisdom or experienced it.

# *Chapter 6*

The Cost of Doing Nothing

I will have everyone missed opportunities please.

Many of us think that if we want to do nothing, that it is ok. The world works together to give us all opportunities for happiness. The decision to take advantage of those opportunities is up to the individual, but taking advantage of opportunities determines if we are happy or not. Do not sit around waiting. One must make things happen. If a trip to Vegas is on your list, do not sit around and cry about not having enough money to go. Figure out how much it cost and start working overtime, saving money and make it happen. The sun is going to rise rather we get up or not, but for those of us who want to see the beauty of the sunrise, we have to get up.

Think about it, we all know the hard workers because they work hard. Do not tell everyone about your dreams, go out and live them and then everyone will see the person living their dreams. If one does not know what his or her dreams are at this point in this book, stop now and write them down. Do not worry about dreams being too ambitious or too expensive. Find a way. Be self-motivated.

## Some of My Life Experiences

I have lived an extraordinary life, and by my friends or anyone standard they would agree. I have travel to most of the great cities in the U.S. and many exotic places in the world. I owned houses in tropical places like Hawaii, California and Florida. I have been to the Grammys, American Music Awards and got to see the top performers in concerts. I owned cars like Mercedes, Porsche, Escalades and BMW. I have been to the Olympics, the World Series, the NBA Finals, the Super Bowl, the BCS Championships, Rose Bowls, and I even went to the Stanley Cup Finals. I need a new Life List because I have gone through my old list. This can be your life.

There is a reason that I enjoy life, and that is because life taught me valuable lessons early. The main one is to take advantage of life opportunities even if they are someone else opportunities. For example, in 2003, the Super Bowl was in San Diego, and the Raiders made it to the Super Bowl. One of my managers was a San Diego Charger season ticket holder selected to have tickets to the Super Bowl. There was no way she wanted anything to do with the hated Raiders, so she offers me the tickets at face value. I paid $500 per ticket when I would have paid $5,000.

I grew up in Florida watching Tampa Bay play football, and when I went to school at Southern California, the Raiders were playing at the Coliseum, so two teams that I liked were playing, and I got to go for the cost of someone else's opportunity. That is what I mean by saying taking advantage of other people opportunities. Learn from this example and any other that one may encounter. I discover this at a remarkably young age which has allowed me to have a fantastic life.

Another life lesson I learned was when I was a freshman in college. I met this girl walking to class. Her dorm was right next to mines, and her morning class was close to mine. We walked the same way every day. One day, I said something to her and since that day, we walked to class every day. It was obvious that she liked me. Some of my female friends that I went to high school with and now the same college became extremely upset because the girl was a different race. They even started to walk me to class. Naturally, the girl gets put off by my friends and she stopped walking with us.

About six months later, one of the guys from my dorm started to date this girl. The tough part was when he told us how passionate she was. She would cook for him, and they would have sex all the time. I thought that happiness is mines, and I lost it to not my prejudice, but the prejudices of my friends. I promise myself that I would not let someone else get all the happiness that is for me. In fact, if I saw someone else letting their chance at happiness get away, I was going to take their happiness.

We all know people who died way too soon. Do not wait until retirement. One may spend all their retirement going to the hospital and making doctor appointments. That person will be regretting that he or she waited to enjoy life. The exciting thing is that one can start enjoying life right now. An individual just have to decide what enjoyment is, and write it down so that he or she does not forget!

Side rant: I remember doing the heyday of the mortgage boom, we were so busy that we could work 20 hours days and still have a lot of work to do. I remember calling traders in New York at midnight New York time and having them answer the phones. I was the Vice President of the Western Region, and I liked to meet with my managers once a quarter. I remember having every one of my managers call me and ask if we could cancel the meeting because they were too busy to come. That is when I notice the burn out and the sadness of my managers. Some of them were making as much as fifty thousand dollars a month, and they were miserable. That did not make any sense. Who would not be happy making that much money?

I then told my manager that not only would I not cancel the quarterly meeting, but I am going to change it to a monthly meeting, and it will be mandatory. What they did not know is that I was changing it from a boring meeting to a fun event each month. For example, the Lakers made it to the NBA finals, and I had a suite for the finals, so I took the managers and their spouses or significant others to the NBA finals. I think the spouses were even more excited than my managers.

One of my offices was in Hawaii, so I held one of the monthly meetings in Hawaii which compose of a meeting dinner with their spouses or significant others and they rest of the time they got to enjoy Hawaii.

One time, I took my managers to New York so that they could meet the traders on the trading floor. It coincided with the Yankees making the World Series, so we had to go to the World Series. The point is that they were so busy that I had to make them have fun and enjoy their lives.

I later required them to hang up pictures of what they wanted in life and when they got it, they could take down the pictures. If I came by their office, I would ask them where their pictures are. Many of them bought dream houses and multiple luxury cars. I began to see smiling and happy managers along with their happy families.

One of my manager that lived in Hawaii got cancer. The day before he died, he sent me a text thanking me for making him enjoy life. He had bought this dream house by one of the most beautiful beaches in Hawaii. Every time I went there he would have a tremendous barbeque, and afterward, we would go to the beach. He had gotten cancer before he turned 40 years old. None of us knows how long we have left on this Earth. A good piece of advice is to enjoy your life NOW!!!

### Life Math Function (Could Have + Would Have + Should Have = Did Not).

Another Law of the Universe is a person can only live in one time. Anyone who lives in the past cannot live in the present or the future. One has to decide where he or she is going to live. If a person is always reliving the past, it will be difficult, if not impossible, to live in the present. All your energy focuses on the past. The present is not in your focus. On the other hand, the person that lives in the future is a dreamer.  He or she is always thinking about tomorrow.  Those three things; past, present and future are the same as yesterday, today and tomorrow.  Gone is yesterday, no one can go back to yesterday; let it go.  Tomorrow never comes, so a person will be waiting forever trying to live in tomorrow.   The only logical choice is to live in the present or today.

I remember losing the first girl that I fell in love with in college.  She wanted to get married right after college and being a 21 year old single guy; marriage was the last thing on my mind.  She kept telling me that she wanted to get away and start a new life, but I was not paying attention.

I remember going to a club one night and meeting this hot red head girl who invited me to go home with her after the dance.  I did, and she was as wild as her hair.  I mean scratches on the back and everything.  She was a screamer too.  She told me her story of how she lives in the back house of her father residence, and she hated her father. They fought about everything.  She even said that he was racist and would not be extremely happy to see me with her.  She also told me that he owned a collection of guns.  I remember leaving that night thinking that I could have gotten shot.  She called me the next night and said to come over.  I remember driving over thinking this is crazy.  What if the father shoot me and say he thought that I was a burglar, but my mind kept going back to the fact that I was going to have some wild and crazy sex (totally worth the risk by the way).

So this went on for about six months until the girl that I thought I would be eventually marrying told me that she was moving out of state.  By chasing temptation (wild redhead), I lost sight of what was the most valuable thing to me. After the girl that I loved left, I stop seeing the red head. No way would I marry someone with so much hatred. I spent the next few years working my way to the top. Eventually, the girl I loved came back into my life, but she was not the same person. Some guy had sucked all the life out of her, and she was in her man hating stage. I could not even get her to say she love me anymore, when she would say it all the time before.

If I could go back in time, I would have married her and had an extraordinary life and family together, but that is life or should I say life math function. Know what one wants so when one gets it, he or she will know it. Write it down in case one forgets. So guys and girls, if we have that dream person, stop making it a nightmare, live the dream! If the individual does not have that dream person, write down all the hurtful things that current person did in your relationship and look at the list every time that person tries to get back into your life.

There are more life stories that I could share, but I think that everyone gets the point. What does a lost day cost? It is immeasurable! How much does one think a lost year cost? Do not find out. Live for the now! Do not wait for some life threatening event to happen. Go out and do what one wants to do now. Remember, love and time are two of the most valuable things in the world and everyone has them both. Focus on spending time loving Your Universe. I used to tell my overworked managers all the time, if they died, my bosses will ask me one question; whom will I replace them with? The job will not stop because an individual takes some time for him or herself. Try it. Make your Life List or Life Goals and spend each day doing them or working on doing them and that makes for a happy life.

# Chapter 7

## __Taking Crazy 101 & 102__

The number one rule in a relationship is that if you have a dog, you will be dealing with crap!

We all heard the definition of insanity as "doing the same things and expecting different results"[4]. Crazy 101 is when someone makes a decision that a normal person would not make, and Crazy 102 is when he or she becomes an expert at it. We have all been in relationships where we knew it was going to end. The other person did not treat us well. In fact, they treated us like they did not like us, but we stuck it out until we reached a breaking point. After all that, they shed some tears, and we take them back. That is taking crazy 101 and 102, accepting an unhealthy relationship when one knows it is unacceptable. Remember one of the Laws of the Universe, "everything has a price", and "Grief is the price we pay for love"[5].

I know what everyone is thinking. That person is my "true love", but please do not forget one extremely powerful thing; for it to be true love, that person has to return love; otherwise it is just stalking (just kidding). If that person does not return love, it is not true love by definition. Do not be Dummy2! People know when the other person loves them. They cannot wait to see the person. Think about it; how happy people are to see their children, parents or someone that they love? People know love when they see it. A person in love will tell that person every day. They will light up when he or she comes into the room. They will not treat that person like dirt or do everything they can to avoid spending time with them. If a person had a choice of late nights at work or coming home to the one that he or she loves, which one would they choose? We know what love look like so only keep those who love the individual on your planet. One way to ensure a happy life is to surround your-self with nothing, but people who love the individual. We have to end relationships that do not have love flowing both ways.

I remember hearing that Bill Withers song, "Use me"[6]. The verse that says "my friend think that it is their appointed duty to tell me" says a lot because it is your friends and family appointed duty to protect the people they love. If trusted friends are saying that some person is not suitable, one should take a hard look at that relationship. Everyone should be able to understand this after reading this book. Look at the way the other person behaves. Are theirs the action of someone in love?

**"I am Love's bitch"**

Guess what is next! Keep a list of all the hurtful things in these questionable relationships. When these people want to go out, look at the list. I swear this works. I had an ex-girlfriend that begged me every day to get back together. I would talk to her on the phone and agree to go out with her on a date. Afterward, I would pull out my list and remember all the hurtful things she did in the relationship, and I would call her back and cancel the date. It kept me from being Dummy2.

If someone loves a person then that list will be short but if someone is in a bad relationship, seeing it written on paper will make it real. Remember, "For every little thing that you hold onto, you have to let something else go"[7]. So if one is holding onto a bad relationship, he or she is letting good relationships go. I know that everyone is thinking that all relationships have problems, but those that are true love can overcome any problems. I remember a saying from

Bob Marley "The truth is that everyone is going to hurt you, you just got to find the ones worth suffering for"[8]. We are all human and all make mistakes, but we should know what love looks like.

Remember, Love is one of the most valuable things on this Earth. It is even more valuable than time.

## Building Stronger Relationships with Your Universe

Please do not believe that this book wants everyone to examine every relationship. In fact, the main purpose of the book is to help everyone to build stronger relationships with Your Universe. We all have heard the story of what happen when a moth sees a flame. We just want to make sure that the individual is the flame of the relationship and not the moth.

Wise people truly believe that a strong relationship with Your Universe will make everyone happy. So guess what, we have a list to help do that. A person needs to know not only what makes them happy but what makes your Universe happy. Look at Life Survey (YU) –Your Universe – and talk to the people in your life and find out what they like. How can a person get their best friends the best gifts if he or she does not know what they like? How can a person send their mom her favorite flowers if he or she does not know what they are?

A true story, I once dated a girl whose mom hated roses! She fell into some rose bushes when she was a kid and got scratched up pretty bad. Mother's day came around, and I thought that I was being a good boyfriend by surprising her mother with roses. All I had to do is asks my girlfriend what were her favorite flowers. I am sure she would have told me the mother in the rose bushes story. Trust me, ask the questions! I do not know where your friends and family ended up on your Focus List, but if they are high on your list, make time to know and enjoy them.

This book point is to use the wisdom of the past and most of us have a ton of wisdom available to us and we do not know it. That is right, your parents and grandparents. It was a long held tradition that the elders in the family imparted their wisdom to the younger generation. Do not let all the wisdom in your family go to the grave with them.

In chapter eight, one will find Life Survey (WI) – Wisdom Interview – this list is for the wise people in your life. I remember doing a wisdom interview on my mother as preparation for this book. I even video tapped it so that I could share it with the rest of the family. She said things that I would have never thought especially on the life regret question. While everyone can make up their own questions, I added things toward the end of the form like what is their favorite things to receive and what are their top songs of all times.

The reason is that the individual is going to do something with those questions. It is going to be a payment for their life wisdom. For example; the questions goes like this - what gifts does your wisdom person like to receive the best, cash, flowers, surprise gifts, or other things? Whatever they say, that is the gift that the individual is going to give them. Think about it, your parents or grandparents tell what make them happy, and the individual has a chance to make them happy, we have to do it!

The last question asks them to list their favorite songs of all times. The individual is going to take that list and download those songs on a computer, music player or tablet so they can listen to their favorite songs anytime. I still have video of me teaching my mother how to play videos on YouTube. That was a truly proud moment for me. The thing is to teach them how to use the music player, tablet or computer (buy one if they do not have one because they are worth it).

The parents and grandparents give us so much; this is one way that we can repay them. If the individual does not know computers either, have your kids teach them. The music player may be an easier option although those screens are small. Just imagine the smile on your grandparents faces when they watch their favorite group singing right there in their bedroom. All this technology is available to them. They just need us to bring it to them. I promise it will bring both them and the individual immense joy to see your parents and grandparents happy. One may even be able to introduce them to your favorites groups. Imagine taking your parent to a concert by your favorite band. I still remember taking my mom to a Lakers game in my Lakers Suite.

## GOD

Building a strong relationship with God is vital. If one becomes this divine person who live an exciting life on earth, but he or she ends up in the wrong place after death; this book is not doing its job. We have to choose a side! Either an individual believes in God or not. What does it hurt to spend some time investing in believing in God? Decide on your own; do not just follow people. Think about it, different cultures who all spoke different languages all believed in

God, so the thought that this idea spread is not right. These people no matter what language they spoke or where they were from knew that there was a God. As mention earlier in the book, everyone is going to be dead way longer than he or she is alive, make sure that the individual place of death will be a pleasant one.

The belief that God will help us get through tough times will keep people going even when life tells them to give up. All who believes in God have stories of when faith carried us when otherwise we would not have made it. Trust me that in building a strong relationship with God will make everyone a better person.

## Love is everything

"I am sorry, but I cannot marry you. I just met you tonight".

Love can no longer be a four letter word. That is why so many relationships end. The expectation of being in love is so small compared to what it should be. We all watched the comedy where two stranger look at each other across a room and declare that it is love at first sight. Six months later, they are breaking up or getting a divorce.

Why did I choose "Everything"? It is long. So if someone wants to love the individual, the definition of love is "Everything".

## **EVERYTHING**

(E) – A person has to bring **E**motions to the relationship.

(V) – A person has to bring some **V**alue to the relationship.

(E) – A person has to bring some **E**ffort to the relationship.

(R) – A person has to bring **R**espect to the relationship.

(Y) – A person has to bring **Y**ou to the relationship, not your texts or phone calls, but you.

(T) – A person has to give your **T**ime to the relationship.

(H) – We should both be **H**appy in the relationship.

(I) – A person has to have something **I**nvested in the relationship.

(N) – The relationship has to be about **N**ow, not what we did in the past.

(G) – We have to believe in **G**od together.

Side rant – I remember not seeing one of my dear friends for a long time. She lived in Hawaii and I stopped going there every month. In fact, it had been almost six months since I had last been there. I called her up when I went to Hawaii to sell one of my rental properties. She wanted to meet for dinner. I see her inside the restaurant and I go in to meet her. She gives me this extremely passionate long hug that lasted for several minutes. When we finally stopped the embrace, the lady that was behind us had an enormous smile on her face and said to us; "I felt that hug from back here; you two must love each other". The point is that not only we knew we loved each other, but people witnessing us together know we loved each other. Everyone should know when someone still loves them. It should not be a secret or puzzle that one has to figure out. I can see the question going like this:

Do you love me?

A. Yes
B. No
C. Maybe
D. Guess

People do not have to pick "EVERYTHING", but pick something that is super long and include all the things that one wants and needs in a relationship, especially a lifelong relationship. Pick Supercalifragilisticexpialidocious[9] if a person wants; just do not make it a four letter word. We all deserve better; we deserved to be loved the right way. Everyone may not know what true love is, but they certainly know what it is not. In Your Universe, the individual sets the standard for love.

Think about it; a person tells his or her parents that they love them all the time. That person tells their children with ease. If someone cannot say it, then they are not in love. It should not be hard to tell someone. Why be in a relationship just to be in one? The relationship should be leading to something better. Ladies, if a guy has been dating a girl for five years and has not proposed, he does not want to get marry; because when a person is in love, he or she wants to be with that person forever. I do not want to break up any relationship. I do not want a girl to feel like her guy only wants her for sex. All guys want sex always. Even if, we think that we want something else, and we get a chance to have sex, guys would change their mind to want sex. That is just how guys are.

I am going to reveal men secret. I am going to use a football analogy. If a team wins a game 3 to 0, the team still celebrates the win. They would prefer to win 30 to 0, but a win is a win. Sex can be like that with men. Men would like to win by a touchdown (sex), but if they win by a field goal (blowjob) or safety (hand job), they still win. I know sometime ladies do not feel like having a guy all over them; however I can tell ladies that if the lady let us kick field goals or score safeties, men will be happy. Trust me happy men do not usually go out and cheat. If the lady shows emotions and makes it sexy by saying things like "I love you" while she is doing it, she may only be doing it for a minute or two.

Love is one of the most valuable things in the world. There is nothing a person would not do for love. We have all been love fool, so we know that is true. At what point do we stop being a fool and become a wise person? When do we get a master degree in love? If this book taught the individual anything, it is the fact that the world is yours. God gave the Earth to us, act like we own the Earth and go live your life with the ones that the individual loves in the time that we have.

## Standard of Friends (SOF)

Which friend is the standard on which one judges other friends? Like everything else, we must set standards for friends. There has to be a minimum standard whereby one calls someone your friend. The mailman who says "hi" each day is nice, but he is not your friend. We all should have that close friend who by which all other friends must compare. The opposite also holds true for Quick Sand Friends (QSF). These are the friends that are going down and taking people with them, and of course we all have a close friend who turned out to be a Crap Friend. The key thing in life is to have your standards and know who is in which standards. The individual needs to know who would take a bullet for them and who would shoot or stab them in the back.

Ok, we have a few more surveys. These are fun lists. The next Life Survey that the individual has to do is Life Survey (RI) – Relationship Interviews. This survey is for those who are in a relationship with someone. There are two surveys, (RI1) and (RI2). The first one (RI1) is for anyone in a relationship. It asks general questions, but questions one should know the answers to if he or she is in a relationship. Please review Life Survey (RI1) in chapter eight or on the website at www.talktothebook.com.

Side Rant – I had a friend that had asked for my opinion on a real estate issue that she had. She knew that I was an expert in real estate, so she valued my opinion. She wanted me to look over some papers, and she had just moved by the beach. I told her that I used to live in that city, and my favorite restaurant was still there. She suggested that we meet there, and of course I am happy to go to my favorite restaurant. We met and had a lovely dinner and I gave her advice on handling her issue. She called me a couple of days later and had some more questions and wanted to meet for dinner again, but this time we would go to her favorite restaurant. After dinner, we went for a walk on the beach. She started to ask me about marriage and kids. I say that I am still recovering from the recession. In addition, my new job has me traveling out of town three weeks out of the month. There is no way that I am thinking about marriage now.

I am driving home after dinner, and I get a text from her saying that we have to break up because she wants someone who wants to get married. I am thinking, break up; I did not even know we were dating. Now while, my situation was extreme, being on the same page in a relationship is a must! One person cannot think that they are free to date, and the other person is planning the wedding. Bare minimum is to be on the same page where both agree on the status of the relationship, and the best way to make sure is to ask questions by completing the Life Survey form for relationships in chapter eight or on the website at

www.talktothebook.com.

**"Does green means Go?"**

Life Survey (RI2) is for married couples or couples considering marriage. These are deep and life deciding questions so if someone is in a new relationship, do not chase the other person away by going too deep too early. I do not recommend (RI2) questions for anyone in a relationship for less than two months. Here is the fun part, at the end of interview questions, the individual is going to sing their significant other favorite song (lip sing if one has an awful voice). However, if the individual feels that your love one did not answer the questions honestly, then they must sing your favorite song. Lastly, if the individual reacts poorly to one of their answers then both must sing a love duet! If that does not bring two people back together, I do not know what will. Please do Life Survey (RI2) with your significant other.

## The Bitter Pill

We all get sick and have to take those bitter pills, but we know that by taking those pills, we will feel better; relationships are like that. We all make mistakes and have to own up to them. Just take the medicine and hope the side effects will not be worst. We are going to have tough times, but by being in a relationship, we have committed to working together even if it means that we would have to forgive the other person and take the bitter pill.

I wish everyone good luck in your self-improvement quest! I hope that I gave everyone a lot of useful tools to use. Please check out the website www.talktothebook.com. Everyone can get all the forms in this book and other tools to help your development. Remember to live each day as if it is yours! We now know that Life, Love and Time are the most precious things in the world, what we do with that knowledge is up to us. Do not wait for a life altering event to happen, live for the now. We will never be twenty one again! If we wasted that year, we cannot get it back. How many more years can we afford to waste? We cannot get those days back, and when love ones die; we cannot spend time with them. There is someone, somewhere happy in this world; that someone should be "You". "Remember this; that someone, who stops you from doing the things that you want to do should never be **YOU**".

Thanks for buying my book and have an extraordinary life! All the surveys, forms and lists that everyone needs to guide your life are in the next chapter. We also have the forms on the website at www.talktothebook.com.

# Chapter 8

**Life Surveys, Questionnaires and Forms**

1. Life Survey (SE1) – Self Evaluation 1

2. Life Survey (SE2) – Self Evaluation 2

3. Life Cycle

4. Life Survey (FS1) & (FS2) – Friend Survey & Family Survey

5. Life Survey (PL) – Problems List

6. Life Survey (LF) – Life Focus

7. Life Survey (LL) – Life List or Life Goal

8. Life Survey (FL) – Fun List  (AKA Happy Next List)

9. Life Survey (YU) – Your Universe

10. Life Survey (WI) – Wisdom Interview

11. Life Survey (RI1) – Relationship Interview 1

12. Life Survey (RI2) – Relationship Interview 2

13. Life Survey (MED) – Medical tracking form

14. Life Survey (DH) – Define happy list

# Life Survey (SE1)

Self-Evaluation

You

| **Positive** | **Need to Improve** |
|---|---|
| 1. _____ | 1. _____ |
| 2. _____ | 2. _____ |
| 3. _____ | 3. _____ |
| 4. _____ | 4. _____ |
| 5. _____ | 5. _____ |

For every need to improve thing, one must have a positive thing.  Do not put more than five items each.  Everyone should have some positive things about him or herself that they do not have to improve.

After listing the need to improve items, list the ways to improve them.

1. _____
   _____
   _____
2. _____
   _____
   _____
3. _____
   _____
   _____
4. _____
   _____
   _____
5. _____
   _____
   _____
6. _____
   _____
   _____
7. _____
   _____
   _____
8. _____
   _____
   _____
9. _____
   _____
   _____
10. _____
    _____
    _____

# Life Survey (SE2)

Self-Evaluation 2

You Now                                   Ideal You

Height –                                   Height –

Weight –                                   Weight –

Appearance –                               Appearance –

Worker –                                   Worker –

Life –                                     Life –

Friends –                                  Friends –

Family –                                   Family –

God –                                      God –

Take a look at the items.  Now write below how one is going to get to the "Ideal You".

1. _____

2. _____

3. _____

4. _____

5. _____

6. _____

7. _____

8. _____

## Life Cycle

**Life Cycle**

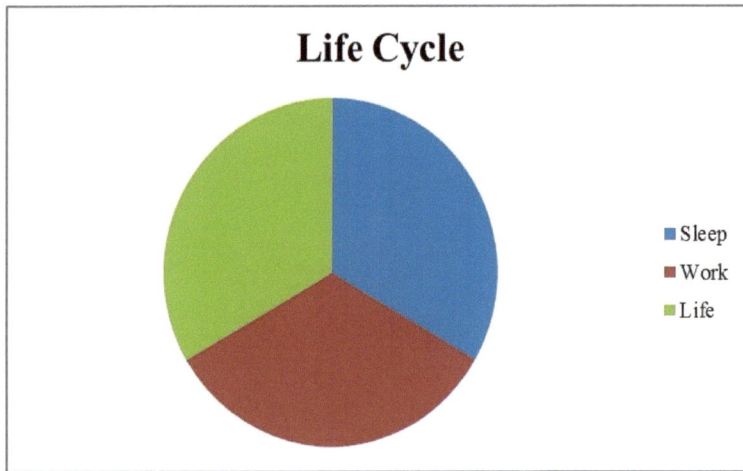

1. How many hours on average for sleep _____ Work _____ Life ____? Total must equal 24 hours.

   Ways to get back in balance. Try to max work at 8 hours!

   **Life Cycle**

   1. _____

   2. _____

   3. _____

   4. _____

   5. _____

   6. _____

   7. _____

   8. _____

# Life Survey (FS1) - Friends Feedback

1. What kind of person do you think that I am?
   A. Positive
   B. Negative
   C. Neutral
   D. Assume crash position

2. Would you say that I am a _____?
   A. Giver
   B. Taker
   C. Other, please describe
   D. I do not know

3. Do you think that I am a spiritual person?
   A. Yes
   B. No
   C. Other, please describe
   D. I do not know

4. Would you call me a family person?
   A. Yes
   B. No
   C. Other, please describe
   D. I do not know

5. What type of friend do you think I am?
   A. Great
   B. Good
   C. Bad
   D. I do not know

6. Would you say that I have a _____ life?
   A. Happy
   B. Sad
   C. OK
   D. I do not know

7. How would you rate my overall appearance?
   A. Beautiful
   B. OK
   C. Bad
   D. Do not ask, Do not tell

8. What kind of worker do you think I am?
   A. Workaholic
   B. Hard worker
   C. Average worker
   D. Lazy worker

9. When listing your friends, where do I rank?
   A. Best friend
   B. Close friend
   C. Friend
   D. Not really a friend

10. What are some things that I could do to improve myself?

# *Life Survey (FS2) Family Feedback*

1. What kind of person do you think that I am?
   - A. Positive
   - B. Negative
   - C. Neutral
   - D. Assume crash position

2. Would you say that I am a _____?
   - A. Giver
   - B. Taker
   - C. Other, please describe
   - D. I do not know

3. Do you think that I am a spiritual person?
   - A. Yes
   - B. No
   - C. Other, please describe
   - D. I do not know

4. Would you call me a good family person?
   - A. Yes
   - B. No
   - C. Other, please describe
   - D. I do not know

5. What type of family member do you think I am?
   - A. Great
   - B. Good
   - C. Bad
   - D. I do not know

6. Would you say that I have a _____ life?
   - A. Happy
   - B. Sad
   - C. OK
   - D. I do not know

7. How would you rate my overall appearance?
   - A. Beautiful
   - B. OK
   - C. Bad
   - D. Do not ask, Do not tell

8. Have I been a good family member to you?
   - A. Yes
   - B. No
   - C. Sometimes
   - D. I would like to take a pass on this one

9. Where do I rank as far as a family member in this family?
   - A. One of the best
   - B. In the middle
   - C. Toward the bottom
   - D. Not sure

10. What are some things that I could do to improve myself?

**<u>Life Survey (PL) – Problems List</u>** - Problems in life to take care of (start with only a few to begin with).

Problem

1. _____

   _____

Solution

1. _____

   _____

Problem

2. _____

   _____

Solution

2. _____

   _____

Problem

3. _____

   _____

Solution

4. _____

   _____

## <u>Life Survey (LF) – Life Focus</u>

## *Life Focus (what is #1)*

What are the most valuable things in your life?  This will guide your life and give one focus!

Life Focus

1. _____

2. _____

3. _____

4. _____

5. _____

6. _____

7. _____

8. _____

9. _____

10. _____

## Life Survey (LL) – Life List or Life Goals (TBDB – To be done by)

Life Events to Go To                    Date completed or TBDB

1. _____     _____

2. _____     _____

3. _____     _____

4. _____     _____

5. _____     _____

6. _____     _____

7. _____     _____

8. _____     _____

9. _____     _____

10. _____     _____

## Life Survey (LL) – Life List or Life Goals

Life Places to go to.                    Date completed or TBDB

1. _____    _____

2. _____    _____

3. _____    _____

4. _____    _____

5. _____    _____


Life Major Things to Do                  Date completed or TBDB

1. _____    _____

2. _____    _____

3. _____    _____

4. _____    _____

5. _____    _____

## Life Survey (FL) – Fun List or Happy Next List

Fun List (Happy Next List)                    Picture of Events

1. _____    _____

2. _____    _____

3. _____    _____

4. _____    _____

5. _____    _____

6. _____    _____

7. _____    _____

8. _____    _____

9. _____    _____

10. _____    _____

# Life Survey (YU) – Your Universe

## Your Sun

1. Name _____

2. Name _____

3. Name _____

4. Name _____

## Your Universe

1. Name _____  13. Name _____

2. Name _____  14. Name _____

3. Name _____  15. Name _____

4. Name _____  16. Name _____

5. Name _____  17. Name _____

6. Name _____  18. Name _____

7. Name _____  19. Name _____

8. Name _____  20. Name _____

9. Name _____  21. Name _____

10. Name _____  22. Name _____

11. Name _____  23. Name _____

12. Name _____  24. Name _____

## People to move out of "Your Universe" (QSF and Crap Friends)

1. Name _____  5. Name _____

2. Name _____  6. Name _____

3. Name _____  7. Name _____

4. Name _____  8. Name _____

# *The Wisdom Interview*

Use this form to interview your parents, grandparents or someone wise in your life that the individual values their wisdom. No reason, one cannot learn from their mistakes especially if it makes your life easier. Questions nine (9) and ten (10) are for what they want. In question number nine, the individual will write down their favorite songs and either buy them a music player or use the one they have, and put those songs on their music player, so that the individual may give them perfect gifts for the wisdom. In question number ten, who does not like getting things? Give them what they like best! The individual can make up their own questions. Good Luck!

1.  What is your greatest regret in life and why?

2.  What is your greatest joy in life and why?

3.  What are some of your mistakes in life that I should know?

4.  What advice do you have about life for me?

5.  What is your favorite thing to do and why?

6.  Describe the happiest time in your life.

7.  What life lessons are you willing to share with me?

8.  What is your favorite quote or saying?

9.  What are your top ten favorite songs of all time?
    (As payment for the wisdom, the individual will put these songs on a music player, tablet or computer).

10. What does one like getting the most: Flowers, surprise gifts, cash or something else?
    (As payment for the wisdom, the individual will give them what they like getting the most).

11. If one could go back in time and change one thing, what would that be?

12. Make up your own questions.

# Life Survey (RL1) Relationship 1

A relationship depends on communication and both parties being on the same page. These questions are to make sure if the individuals are in a relationship that both persons recognize it.

1. What kind of relationship are we in?
   A. Open non exclusive
   B. Exclusive
   C. Just friends
   D. Soul Mate
2. What is your favorite color?
3. What is your favorite movie?
4. What is your favorite song?
5. What is your favorite gift to get?
6. What is your favorite TV show?
7. What is your favorite Sport or extra-curricular activity?
8. What are your pet peeves?
9. Who is your favorite band?
10. Who is your favorite singer?
11. What is your favorite restaurant?
12. What is your favorite food?
13. Where is your favorite place to vacation?
14. Where do you see yourself in ten years?
15. What is your favorite dessert?
16. What is your idea of a perfect date?
17. What makes you angry?
18. What makes you happy?
19. What makes you sad?
20. What is the most important thing in your life right now?
21. What place would you like to go in the next year?
22. Are you a positive or a negative person?
23. What are your three favorite things to do?
24. Are you a morning or night person?
25. How do you feel about me right now?
26. What is your greatest regret in life?

# *Life Survey (RL2) Relationship 2*

A relationship depends on communication and both parties being on the same page.  These questions are

for serious relationships.  .

1. What kind of relationship or marriage do we have?
   A. We have issues
   B. Just OK
   C. Good but need to work on some things
   D. Soul Mate
2. Do you want to have children or more children?
3. Who is going to keep the children doing work hours (grandparents, nanny, and house wife – potential income loss)?
4. What city do you want to retire in?
5. Are you happy in this relationship?
6. What are the things I do that bothers you?
7. Where do you want to go on the next vacation?
8. What are your top focuses?
9. What can I do better?
10. What are your great regrets in life?
11. Do you want to stay in this relationship?

The individuals know their relationships the best, so make up your own questions.

12. _____

13. _____

14. _____

15. _____

16. _____

## Life Survey (MED) – Medical tracking form

| Tests | Date<br>Targets | Starting Numbers | Date<br>Goal | Measurement 1 | Measurement 2 | Measurement 3 | Measurement 4 |
|---|---|---|---|---|---|---|---|
| Blood Pressure | | | | | | | |
| Blood Sugar | | | | | | | |
| Weight | | | | | | | |
| BMI | | | | | | | |
| Waist Size | | | | | | | |
| Feelings | | | | | | | |
| Temperature | | | | | | | |
| Exercise (Y or N) | | | | | | | |
| | | | | | | | |

1. Blood Pressure – Buy a blood pressure machine. One should be available at any drug store (check your health plan to see if it is covered).

2. Blood Sugar – Check with your health care professional and see if you need to monitor your blood sugar.

3. Weight – Buy a scale and start your weight plan (make the goal realistic).

4. Body Mass Index (BMI) – Buy a monitor online for a few dollars.

5. Waist size – Buy a tape measure and measure yourself according to your plan.

6. Feelings – Track the days that you feel well and not so well, so you can use the feedback to keep you feeling well.

7. Temperature – Buy a thermometer and take your temperature on days the individual does not feel well.

8. Exercise – Remember exercise is required for good health, track it each day.

The process of tracking these numbers each day takes less than ten minutes.

****There is a 7 days tracking form at www.talktothebook.com. ****

## Life Survey (DH) –Define Happiness

What will make the individual happy?

Life

1. _____

2. _____

3. _____

4. _____

Family

1. _____

2. _____

3. _____

Career

1. _____

2. _____

3. _____

Others

1. _____

2. _____

3. _____

4. _____

## Resources

1.      The Bible (King James Version) – "but with God all things are possible"; Matthew 19:26.

2.      Unknown - "Fool me once, shame on you, but fool me twice, shame on me"- The origin of the proverb, "Fool me once, shame on you, and fool me twice, shame on me" is a matter of debate. There are sources that claim its beginnings are with the ancient Chinese, other sources claim it is from Italy. There are also some sources that speculate the proverb may be from the bible, but with different phrasing.

3.      Socrates - "Employ your time in improving yourself by other writings, so that you shall gain easily what others have labored hard for".

4.      Albert Einstein - "doing the same thing and expecting different results".

5.      Elizabeth, Queen II. - "Grief is the price we pay for love".

6.      Withers, Bill (Composer) - Song "Use Me" {B. Withers, Performer}.

7.      Plato - "For every little thing you hold unto, you have to let something else go".

8.      Marley, Bob - "The truth is everyone is going to hurt you; you just got to find the ones worth it.

9.      Mary Poppins {Motion Picture} - Supercalifragilisticexpialidocious, written by Sherman Brothers, sung by Julie Andrews and Dick Van Dyke.

10.   Pictures provided and copyrighted by Dreamstime.com and Author, Tony Johnson.  All images can be found at www.dreamstime.com or www.talktothebook.com.

Picture copyrights and websites

Cover picture by - © Tony J. | www.talktothebook.com

1. Life - © Andreus | Dreamstime.com
2. Love - © Ashestosky | Dreamstime.com
3. Time - © Lidiya | Dreamstime.com
4. Shakespeare (Actor) - © Pcanzo | Dreamstime.com
5. Lady in mirror - © Andre Adams | Dreamstime.com
6. Map - © Bradcollett | Dreamstime.com
7. Raining - © Danil Chepko | Dreamstime.com and © Paul Victor Marian | Dreamstime.com
8. Patient getting shot - © Irina Mazovka | Dreamstime.com
9. Patient the "boss of me" - © Caraman | Dreamstime.com
10. Life Focus - © Seow Ai Ti Angeline | Dreamstime.com
11. Sporting Events Tickets – ©Tony J. | www.talktothebook.com
12. Body is a Holy Temple - © Citrusss08 | Dreamstime.com
13. Body is the world's largest Temple - © Paulus Rusyanto | Dreamstime.com
14. Weight loss program - © Tony J. | www.talktothebook.com
15. Clip board - © Milo827 | Dreamstime.com

Author: Tony J. at age 21.

This is my graduation picture and my life is unraveling.   The camera man would not take my picture until I smile.  I learned that I could go from stressed out to being happy in zero seconds.  I remembered this for the rest of my life, especially when I was not happy.  I could turn on my **instant happy** switch at any time.  All I had to learn is that it was up to me.

Now it is up to the reader, find your **instant happy** switch and press it a lot!

**Remember this; that someone, who stops you from doing the things that you want to do should never be "YOU".**